WAVERLEY® SCOTLAND

Tartan Cloth
Commonplace Notebook

If found, please contact:

WAVERLEY®
SCOTLAND

Tartan Cloth
Commonplace Notebook

Copyright © 2025 Waverley Scotland

Designed in Scotland by Waverley Scotland
31, Six Harmony Row, Glasgow, Scotland G51 3BA
Printed in China, bound with genuine tartan cloth, woven in mills in Great Britain

Our notebooks are manufactured with FSC certified papers from sustainable forests and our cover boards are made of recycled fibres

www.waverley-books.co.uk

Waverley Scotland is proud to work with
Kinloch Anderson Scotland, experts in tartan since 1868,
to produce genuine tartan cloth notebooks and journals

www.kinlochanderson.com

Kinloch Anderson
SCOTLAND